For Jim...

— Dick Emmons

THE RHYMES OF MY LIFE

A Book of Humorous Light Verse

By
DICK EMMONS

Edited By
DON CANHAM

Olympia Sports Press
745 State Circle Dr.
Ann Arbor, MI 48108

THE RHYMES OF MY LIFE

Cover Design, Layout, and Editorial Services
Provided by:
Matthew Gwinn

Images provided by:
Corel© Corporation
Totem Graphics Inc.®
Image Club
Softkey®

Published by Olympia Sports Press
745 State Circle
Ann Arbor, MI 48108

Library of Congress Catalog card Number:
99-075018

ISBN 0-9654263-1-9

Printed in the United States of America

Dedication

The hell with dogs...
My Helen is my best friend!

Table of Contents

From The Editor

Cage Question

When watching basketball, my wife
Admittedly is lost;
She sees a free throw, then inquires
"What do the others cost?"

This book was conceived at a University of Michigan basketball game in 1999. Dick Emmons passed me a small piece of paper with the above verse (scratched in what I determined was English), I have seen better handwriting!

I had heard Dick recite at banquets and dinners for years, and read his verse in several national publications - and often wondered if others appreciated his humor as much as I did. I mentioned to my wife at that basketball game that he should put his verse in a book - and later when I found he had over 600 of his verse in shoe boxes and back pockets, I decided to edit the material for this book.

As some of you know, Humorist Dick Emmons has been called "America's funniest poet" (although he claims not by many). His light verse has appeared in Reader's Digest, The Saturday Evening Post, McCall's, Good Housekeeping, Golf Digest, The Wall Street Journal and others "not numerous to mention," he stated.

A virtual native of Ann Arbor Michigan, Emmons is a former city editor of The Ann Arbor News and former managing editor of The University of Michigan alumni magazine.

Emmons is a graduate of Hillsdale College who served in the U.S. Army in World War II, his weapon being a typewriter and a tongue in cheek.

He and Helen, his wife of 52 years, have two children and three grandchildren.

Emmons, when not writing, is writhing -- on the golf course, where he vows to shoot his age -- on his 120th birthday. In the meantime he shoots his weight.

I hope you enjoy this collection as much as I have. It is a bedside reader that won't put you to sleep.

Don Canham
Editor

Animal Antics

He's A Rare Dale

My dog is smart as he can be;
I have to give him credit;
He'll bring my paper straight to me–
But not until he's read it.

Feline Fact

The household cat is one thing that
Some people feel a dread for–
And, ten times out of ten, theirs are
The laps the cat will head for.

Whine Lines

If Christmas Day, you give the pup
So wanted by your sprites,
You'll also find you've given up
A lot of silent nights.

Hound Sound

My neighbor says this of his dog:
"His bark's worse than his bite."
I don't quite see how that can be–
He practices all night!

Feline Fling

I throw my cat out every night
To spend time with his cult;
I don't use hands for fear he'll bite–
I use a catapult.

Meandering Mollusk

The snail to speed is not inclined,
And here's why he's so slow:
He simply can't make up his mind
Where he should escargot.

Sound Advice

The old canary in the shop
Seemed anything but strong;
His looks were shot, but I cared not—
I got him for a song.

Rodent Report

All squirrels look alike to me;
I cannot tell a he from she,
But, as the squirrels numbers double,
It's clear that they don't have that trouble.

Tooth Truth

The beaver's a hard-working cuss
Whose teeth act like a saw,
But would I want, in my next life,
To be a beaver? Gnaw.

Sad Ending

The canine tail that wags upright
Reveals an inner glow,
But when the thing is lowered, it
Becomes a tail of woe.

Garment Gripe

The penguin's Social Life, alas,
Is anything but normal;
When he's invited, he must pass—
Unless, or course, it's formal.

Booming Business

Whenever thunder splits the air,
My dog gets quite unsteady;
He dives beneath the bed to find
That I am there already.

Aren't Pets A'door'able!

A cat that wants to go outside
Will rub against your shins;
You're napping in your easy chair—
That's when the rub begins.

A dog that wants to go outside
Will poke you in the tibia,
Or, if it is a Newfoundland,
He'll poke you in your ribia.

And once you yield to poke or rub
And settle down again,
The poker and the rubber will
Decide they want back in.

Warren Peace

The mama bunny keeps her young
Close by her, just in case—
She feels unease each time she sees
A hare that's out of place.

Outside Information

A chipmunk lives in our woodpile,
No larger than a splinter;
He's cute as pie and that is why
We had no fires last winter.

Time Trauma

Beyond all birds, the cuckoo should
Be scared out of his socks—
All other predators aside,
He must watch out for clocks.

Fume Fear

The skunk emits a noxious spray,
Then triggers his reloader—
What scares him most is that someday
It may be out of odor.

Airedale Admission

I couldn't get along without
My dog; he's such a riot—
But there are moments, I confess,
When I would like to try it.

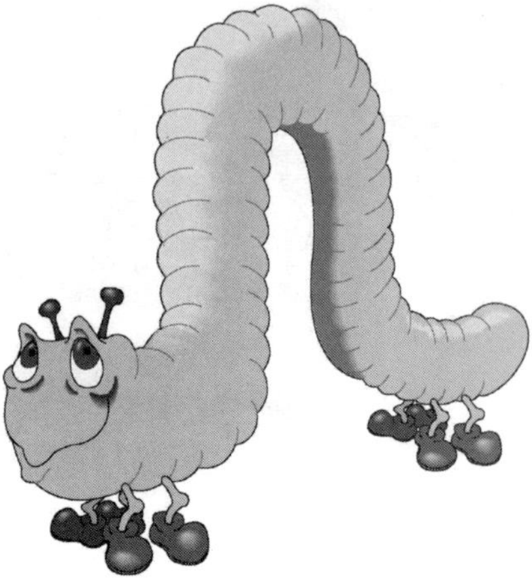

Larval Marvel

God made the caterpillar gross
And ugly to the eye—
Then feeling sorry, let the thing
Become a butterfly.

Foot Note

That polar bears will mate at all,
And, what is more, repeat,
Is quite a thing, considering
Both parties have cold feet.

Gene Job

Of vice the female tern has none,
All evil thoughts she'll smother;
She then gives birth, believing one
Good tern deserves another.

Posthumous Protection

The mink of one thing is assured
(Few others share this trait):
Nine times in ten, he'll be insured—
For him, though, it's too late.

Under Statement

Hear this, you moles beneath my lawn:
What you've done is a crime;
I warn you now you'll soon be gone—
You live on burrowed time.

Amphibian Admission

I've not known many frogs, alas—
We've not laughed, drunk or joked;
I met one in my science class,
But then, of course, he croaked.

Leg Leader

No animal on earth can beat,
For speed afoot, the cheetah—
A few may be almost as fleet,
But nobody is fleetah.

Game Plan

At hunting time, the deer lies low,
On cover he has counted—
He's much too smart, I'll have you know,
To stand up and be mounted.

Aviary Admission

I'm sorry for the dodo bird,
Who's said not to exist—
But I concede that he's a breed
I really haven't missed.

Insect Inquiry

How come we don't respect the moth
When he is, clearly, of the cloth?

Departing Lines

The dinosaur has ceased to be.
That's perfectly all right with me.

Get That Name Changed

Male ladybug, it's up to you,
But, in your place, I think I'd sue.

Rodent Write-Off

I'm very sorry for the rat.
He had no friends. And that is that.

Preferred Pooch

Some dogs catch frisbees thrown at them!
It's really quite a knack—
But I'll hold my applause 'til I
See one that throws it back.

Hint for a Hippopotamus

The hippo is an ugly beast
When going west or going east;
Since that is true of south and north,
The hippo shouldn't sally forth.

Seat Bleat

I put this question to my dog
A dale who has an air:
"What, may I ask, makes Man's Best Friend
Think he owns Man's Best Chair?"

Outside Information

Two cows grazed in a farmer's field
As slowly past I went;
One cow had "Skim" up on her side,
The other "Two percent."

Animal Audit

In wintertime bears hibernate;
That's ALL they do, the experts state;
Permit me to express a doubt:
Two bears went in, four bears came out.

Cover Story

The caterpillar blindly crawls;
His compass seems inferior;
His thinking is as fuzzy, I'm
Afraid, as his exterior.

Sea Shock

So doggone many fish get caught,
I have to think they're fools;
That comes as a surprise because
I thought they lived in schools.

After Glow

The lightning bug will show himself,
Then, just like that, expire;
Who blames him? Would you stick around
If your tail was on fire?

Sting Operation

The two mosquitoes on your Ark,
Dear Noah, prompt me to remark
That life today would be more fun
If you had just invited one.

Revolving Rover

Someday I'm gonna ask my dog,
Who really is a clown,
Why he must turn around three times
Before he can lie down.

Monkey Business

We're all descended from the apes,
Says Darwin and I buy it;
But one thing that you may not know
Is that the apes deny it.

Insect Aside

Because we have computer skills,
We humans think we're clever;
We're not, compared to spiders -- they've
Been on the web forever.

Bottom Lines

We've tried to paper-train our pup,
But, sadly, he just shrugs;
We named him Spot because that's what
He does to all our rugs.

Stinging Remark

Since God made everything there is,
(The Good Book doesn't lie),
He must have made mosquitoes, too --
I'm sure I don't know why.

Aviary Advice

I've just found out that cuckoo birds,
Not wanting to be mothers,
Transfer their eggs to strangers' nests
So they'll be raised by others
Since I'm a parent, too, I guess
This practice should appall;
Instead, I think the cuckoo's not
So cuckoo after all.

Food Fancies

Spud Song

I love potatoes with a love
That simply can't be dashed;
I love them diced, I love them riced
And boiled and baked and mashed.

I think they're neat with any meat,
And that brings me to ham–
Of sweet potatoes am I fond?
The answer's yes, I yam.

Meat Matter

The world's divided in two groups;
The lines are clear, not hazy–
One half (like me) hates liver and
The other half is crazy.

Consummate Condiment

This gastronomic truth just must
Be said before we move on:
There is no food I've ever chewed
That ketchup won't improve on.

Fare Statement

I tried a brand-new restaurant
And gave the place a C;
The food was what I'd call B, but
I'd rate the maitre D.

Consuming Desire

Someday, somewhere, it's my design,
Before I've left this track,
To sniff the cork and taste the wine–
And send the bottle back

Check Choice

When we go out on New Year's Eve,
We gorge on food and wine–
The bill's so fat, quite frankly, that
I just let Auld Lang sign.

Name Game

In restaurants, the better coats
In checkrooms don't repose–
They're always draped on chairs, one notes,
So that the label shows

Roll Report

The bagel's held in such regard,
You don't hear many knocks on it;
In fact, for fear a thief is near,
A lot of us put lox on it.

Biting Comment

Two things are true about hors d'oeuvres:
You do not have to shell 'em,
And it's a whole lot easier,
I find, to eat than spell 'em.

Sound Advice

Italians seem obsessed by food;
Obsessed? Why, holy cow—
They cannot say hello without
Pronouncing it as chow.

Of Courses

Do not eat meat, do not eat spuds,
(The negatives are lots)—
Accordingly, in restaurant,
I go from soup to nots.

Here We Go 'Round the Juniper Bush!

There's no such thing as one martini,
But two can make your posture leany;
And, should you gulp a third and fourth,
East looks like West and Nouth is Sorth;
One guy drank five, much to his sorrow—
The service is at noon tomorrow.

Restaurant Reflection

There is no way to keep, dear chap,
A paper napkin on your lap.

Bacon Lettuce and Tomato

In all the world, Americans
Comprise the only band which
Insists that these three elements
Will stay inside a sandwich.

Eat Bleat

How is it that the waiter rates
His title when it's I who waits?

International Cuisine

Our coffee's from Columbia
And China grows our tea;
Our sauce, of course, is Holland-aise,
Our kraut's from Germany.

Tamales come from Mexico
And Ireland gives us stew—
You ask me where we get our pears?
Well, I suppose Pearu.

Root Report

Some folks plant parsnip, I am told,
Then reap them from each hummock
And eat them boiled or baked or cold—
I find that hard to stomach.

Inside Information

Old-fashioneds are a type of drink
That many prize quite highly;
One gives you glee, but after three,
You just sit and smile ryely.

Breakfast is Eggstasy

I like eggs poached, hard-boiled or shirred;
To fried eggs I'm addicted;
I also like them scrambled and
I *love* them Benedicted!

Delayed Damage

The dinner check is always turned
Face downward, which is done, I've learned,
To keep, if possible, the masses
From choking on their demitasses.

Meal Matter

Our waiter frowns a tiny frown,
It's hours since we first sat down;
We finished dinner long ago
And had three cups of coffee—no,
Amend that figure to read four,
And signalled that we want no more;
The check's been paid, the tip has, too;
What holds us to our chairs like glue?
We may be here until the dawn—
My wife can't get her shoes back on.

Flat Statement

At rest upon its side is where
Good wine should always lie;
And, after several glasses, friend,
There also so should I.

Diminished Dessert

I just adore a petit four
But I have weight to lose,
So I don't eat them anymore--
I'm down to petit two's.

Just Asking, America

Don't think me less than loyal, but
I don't quite understand
Why, when we dine, we always switch
The fork to the right hand.

Sticky Question

Does there exist a cocktail place
So loaded down with class
It's napkins don't approach your face
Together with your glass?

Cheese Challenge

I'm partial to French onion soup,
The taste and texture's dandy,
But I don't order it unless
I have some scissors handy.

Reason to Return

I've been to lots of restaurant
That I'd like to revisit,
Not that the service or the food
Were what you'd call exquisite;
Indeed, of food and service they
Were often quite bereft there—
But what would bring me back are the
Umbrellas I have left there.

Thought for Food

The reason airline pilots sound
So cheery, once we've soared,
Is probably because they ate
BEFORE they came on board.

Condiment Counsel

Here's proof the ketchup bottle hates you:
None comes and then it inundates you.

Tastebuds Tribute

Quite lustily I sing the praise
Of zesty, tasty mayonnaise!
There is no food, I hereby move,
That lots of mayo won't improve;
Than yolks of eggs and oil and vinegar
There isn't any dressing winninger;
I click my heals and shout hurray
Whenever "o" comes after "may"!
As proof of how much folks adore it,
They named a famous clinic for it!

Biting Comment

If you eat too much red meat, you
Are asking for some grief,
But every day I crave filet --
And that, pal, is my beef.

Bread Lines

Since loaves are made from flour dough,
Which adds the pounds I dread,
I hereby pray the Lord will <u>not</u>
Give me my daily bread.

Meat Matter

I'd be a vegetarian
Just like a lot of you
If I could find a vegetable
That grew up saying moo.

Nibble Note

When there's a box of chocolates,
The spouse that I am kin to
Makes sure there isn't one piece that
Has not been bitten into.

Cute Cure

The waitress who has penned her name
On checks -- Sue, Pam or Grace,
Will get more yen if she will then
Not draw a smiling face.

Farewell, Fudge!

My diet makes me give up cakes,
All sorts of tortes I've quit—
Meringue-topped pies said their goodbyes
And the banana split.

Dawn Dispute

Some folks think breakfast without eggs
Is absolutely awful,
And some think the reverse is true,
But I'm inclined to waffle.

Squirt Scenario

My grapefruit loooks so good, I plunge
At once, lest it grow older—
And, in a flash, the beauty's in
The eye of the beholder.

Dining Dilemma

A lot of perils have I known
But here's my topmost crisis:
A menu in a restaurant
That does not list the prices.

Caffeine Curse

When some drink coffee late at night,
All hope of sleep they smother;
Some sleep like babies and, of course,
They're married to each other.

Protection Dejection

When dining out on rainy nights,
I'm here to tell you, fella,
I never fail to leave a tip—
And also my umbrella.

Still Kicking

Card Conquest

The day has come
for which I've prayed:
I beat my grandkids
At "Old Maid"!

Why were they so
Upset with me?
I wouldn't play
Two out of three.

Abbreviated Ambitions

I once sought fame and fortune, but
My lifelong chase is done—
My head I bow; I'll settle now,
Dear friends, for either one.

Further Fodder

Our kids have long since left the nest
To meet life on their terms;
They've cut the string and taken wing—
But we still send them worms.

Salute To Senility

Do you recall when tennis balls
Were nothing else but white?
And when a doc came to your house
To make you feel all right?

Do you recall the running board
And planes that ran by prop?
Or frozen milk that pushed the lid
Two inches off the top?

Is there a rhyme by Burma Shave
Still rattling 'round your head?
If you remember the above,
I fear you're damn near dead.

Outsider Observation

These days, it seems, if you've not had
A bypass operation,
At any social function you
Can't join the conversation.

That's What I Yam

Once I outgrew my beanstalk years,
I sowed wild oats—and how!
I was some pumpkins, but I'm just
A couch potato now.

Photo Fact

Grandparents live in happiness;
They're free at last of strictures,
Excepting that they must posses
A wallet full of pictures.

Age Admission

You say you've just turned forty, friend?
That life has clearly reached its end?
Does forty seem your fire's last ember?
I must confess I can't remember.

Lid Lament

The trouble with men's golden years
Is, simply stated, that you
Will never get another set
Of lashes batted at you.

Old Story

Kids welcome grandparents with cheers
And leap to every lap—
There is, it seems, down through the years,
No veneration gap.

What Burglars?

The younger generations will
By this report be shocked:
Time was, when we did errands, we
Would leave the house unlocked!

Whiskey Wish

I've reached that point in life when it
Would fill my heart with glee
If some clerk in a liquor store
Would ask for my ID.

Bran Plan

When I was young I sowed wild oats—
So wild you couldn't beat 'em!
But times have changed and now I find
That I'm supposed to eat 'em.

Going Concern

Retirement down in Florida
I think I can afford;
What keeps me here? Why, just one fear—
I might get shuffle-bored

Cover Story

The early Romans I applaud
Because they weren't by fitness awed;
When orgies left their tummies fatter,
Thanks to their garb, it didn't matter;
How smart they were, those ancient conquerors—
Thick thighs did not make them go bonkerers!
Fie on aerobics, sit-ups, yoga—
What I need is a Roman toga.

Wrinkle Reaction

Mirror, mirror, on the wall,
My fondest wish if that you'll fall.

Skin Statement

Specific data on my age
I work hard at withholding—
My wrinkles, though, reveal that I
Am thirty-nine and folding.

Generation Rap

I can't stand youths, no, not at all,
Whose skin is taut and peachy,
And who look blank when I recall
Mae West or Don Ameche.

Male Malady

It seems to me from what I see,
That chivalry is rare;
If it's not dead, as some have said,
It's in intensive care.

I Kid You Not!

Our children were okay, I guess,
If not quite what we'd planned;
But having said that, I confess,
Their children are—well, grand!

It Bugs Me

In doctors' waiting rooms I squirm
Amid some other folks infirm;
With all those foreign germs afloat,
(for which I have no antidote),
I'll get some pox, just sure as sin,
I didn't have when I came in.

Puppet Tear

I'm sorry for young folks today,
I truly am, by golly;
They've never heard a single word
From Kukla, Fran and Ollie.

Old Story

With age, one's memory grows worse;
Here's proof mine has declined:
I had a last line for this verse,
But it has slipped my mind.

Wet Peeve

I've always had a set of knees
That go out of their way to please;
They've not been damaged on the gridiron,
They're sturdy when I swing a midiron;
When I proposed, the knee I fell on
Was one that I felt really swell on;
All down the years, through thin and thick,
No knee of mine could be called trick;
Although I have some weaker points,
They don't include my legs' large joints;
But my granddaughter, diaper-free,
Dispelled the myth of perfect knee;
For, when I bounced the child upon it,
I instantly got water on it.

Sound Reasoning

My hearing's gone a little flat,
Not fully, just a touch—
But sixty years have taught me that
I am not missing much.

Nodding Doing

About one-thirty, maybe two
A nap is what I wish to do;
I feel like I've been hit, post-luncheon,
By someone with an axe or truncheon;
The world can go downhill on skids
As long as I can close my lids;
Revile me as a lout and loafer,
But go away. I want my soafer.

Pedal Pout

I ride a stationary bike
Some excess pounds to pare—
The bike won't move, of course, nor am
I getting anywhere.

Pillow Talk

I won't reveal how old I am
Because I'm vain and fickle,
But I recall the days when the
Tooth Fairy left a nickel.

Reprieve Report

I count it as a special day,
One truly free of blame,
When I have read the obit list
And did not see my name.

Maintenance Matters

Preservatives in food, I'm told
Make dietitians' blood run cold;
But, at my age, I humbly plead,
Preservatives are what I need.

Natal Note

The day that I turned thirty was
Enough to make me quake,
Then fifty passed and birthdays now
Are just a piece of cake.

Manners Matter

I tipped my hat and held the door
For her (not being lazy),
But, since she was just twenty-four,
She thought that I was crazy.

Garden Varieties

Growing Pains

A thousand different bugs attack
My flowers and my shrubs;
No longer will I break my back–
My garden's up for grubs.

Flower Power

When gardening, I have one gift
You won't find in the manuals:
I know it's strange, but I can change
Perennials to annuals.

Garden Gripe

The inchworm moves quite cleverly,
Thus earning my regard–
But what I mind is when I find
Him measuring my yard.

Lofty Thought

The Lord above sees everything
Beneath the moon and sun,
And that includes my garden, which
Is where His wilt be done.

Tell Me No Lice

Poor little bug upon my plant,
Will you bring on a blight?
You look so tiny that you can't—
But, then again, you mite.

Leaf Grief

A stately oak in our yard keeps
The hot sun off our heads,
And, while that's great, it's also true
That, once it shades, it sheds.

Midsummer Day's Dream

I want, more than power
Or wealth in the bank,
A mower that starts on
The very first yank.

Flower Glower

My Spring bulbs brought my yard alive!
Oh, what a labyrinth!
But rabbits came, alas, and I've
Not see a hyacinth

Hare Fare

The carrots, peas and beans I sowed
And nourished in the rows I hoed
Apparently have come to rest in
Some bunny rabbit's large intestine;
He would have eaten more, no doubt,
Except my Brussels didn't sprout.

Rhyme Reward

Recite some poetry to plants,
I'm told, to make their growth advance;
I therefore read Elizabeth Barrett
To every daff and rose and carrot;
Elizabeth, at you I'm frowning—
I got the same thing you did: browning.

Outside Information

I mow and feed and hoe and weed,
Clean eaves and chop some wood—
At dusk, I'm ready to concede
A condo's looking good.

It's Beastly!

My yard is practically a zoo
Of squirrels and there scions,
Plus woodpeckers and chipmunks, too,
And lots of dandy lions.

Seed Sorrow

Whatever goes up must come down,
From that rule there's no pardon,
But what goes down *may* not come up—
I'm thinking of my garden.

Growing Concern

Thanks to the aphids,
Grubs and mites,
I call my garden
Withering Heights.

Garden Grin

We modern men are urbanites;
We live with locks and clocks;
There are no shepherds in the fields,
But I still tend my phlox.

Pardon My Garden

When Summer's last rose finally
Has in my back yard burst,
I cry a lot 'cause, like as not,
It also is my first.

Nothing Doing

My climbing roses do not climb;
That's not the only slap:
My johnny-jump-ups do not jump,
Nor do my dragons snap.

Fairway Fables

General Custer

George Custer lost his biggest match
And I can see what downed him:
The problem was his foes were in
Red figures all around him.

Jesse James

I never golfed with Jesse James
But I am here to state,
Whatever else you thought of him,
His takeaway was great

Sir Lancelot

Sir Lancelot had a bad round
Which might have made him mad
Except his was a lower score
Than what Sir Galahad.

Pinocchio

The nose of dear Pinocchio
Grew to outrageous size
Because, round after round, he kept
Improving on his lies.

Cleopatra

Queen Cleopatra never golfed,
According to my file–
Apparently she never thought
That it was worth her wile.

Samuel Colt

Colt had the highest handicap
Of any man alive–
The maximum is 40 but
They gave Colt 45.

Achilles

Achilles' round just made him sick,
He had no touch, no feel–
But then he sank a monstrous putt,
Which made Achilles heal.

Adam

When Adam botched things on the tee,
He wouldn't pout or grieve—
He'd smile and go straight home, where he
Looked forward to his eve.

Four Painters

VanGogh, Renoir, Degas, Monet
Drove golf balls in succession–
No records fell, but, what the hell,
They made a good impression.

Henry Ford

When Henry Ford duck-hooked a drive,
He never swore, not he–
Indeed, it may be said he was
A Model on the T.

Old King Cole

With reference to Old King Cole,
Forget all you've been taught–
He took up golf and soon was not
As merry as you thought.

Sir Walter Raleigh

Sir Walter was not playing well,
His game was in a valley,
And yet his fans did not lose hope–
They'd seen Sir Walter Raleigh.

Confucius

Confucius took a vicious swing
And knocked it out of play—
Be grateful, friend, that you did not
Hear what Confucius say.

Jules Vern

Jules Vern had reason to despair
About golf's long delays—
For instance, there was one round where
It took him 80 days!

Narcissus

At first, Narcissus claimed his game
Was very near perfection—
But later he confessed that it
Was not, upon reflection.

Tarzan

When Tarzan's drives went in the woods,
Escaping he knew how to—
His skill in trees, one quickly sees,
Is something we should bough to.

Michelangelo

For trick shots, Michelangelo
Had an uncanny knack—
He made some of his greatest strokes
While lying on his back.

Guglielmo Marconi

Marconi had no luck, you see,
Although his work was tireless—
His shots all wound up near a tree,
Unstaked and, therefore, wireless.

Toulouse Lautrec

Toulouse Lautrec was probably
Not suited to our sport—
I don't know if he underclubbed,
But he was always short.

Jerome Kern

The play of Kern, first name Jerome,
Seemed sure to cop the prize!
Alas, his golf foe lit a pipe—
And smoke got in his eyes.

Napoleon

Napoleon shot awful scores
And why was this the norm?
He wouldn't take his other hand
Out of his uniform.

Morpheus

Invited for a round of golf,
Did Morpheus just leap on it?
Well, it's my guess, instead of "Yes,"
He said he'd have to sleep on it.

Ferdinand Magellan

When Ferdinand Magellan golfed,
The burden that he bore
Was that he played from spots where man
Had never been before.

Gabriel Fahrenheit

There was no course that Fahrenheit
Could bring right to its knees—
His game was terrible, but it
Got better by degrees.

Abraham Lincoln

We can't ask Lincoln how he scored
Because he's now in heaven;
All that we know is that one time
He sighed "Fourscore and seven."

Carry Nation

When Carry Nation played, she was
Unpopular, poor soul;
She might have been accepted, but
She closed the nineteenth hole.

Marshall Field

When Marshall Field played the first hole,
He'd make an awful score,
But little did his golf foes know
What good things lay in store!

Mickey Mouse

When Mickey Mouse went to the tee,
His shots were wildly struck;
No one could say where they might stray
And that made Donald duck.

The Sheik of Araby

The sheik of Araby looked great
When he strode to the tee!
His swing brought woe, of course, but oh,
The chic of Araby!

Knute Rockne

Knute Rockne had his clubs regripped;
The new ones made him chipper—
His game renewed, in gratitude
He won one for the gripper.

Louisa May Alcott

The Alcott called Louisa May
Gave every foe a trimmin'—
Her record, though, is marred since she
Played only little women.

Houdini

Houdini didn't score as well
As lots of other chaps,
But he was absolutely swell
At getting out of traps.

Beethoven, Brahms and Chopin

Beethoven, Brahms and Chopin played
A threesome, I'm confidin'—
Although they tried to find a fourth,
The guy was always Haydn.

Mona Lisa

When Mona Lisa golfed, she had
Of willing partners few—
She'd hit it out of bounds and smile
And Louvre it up to you.

Franz Lehar

Franz Lehar played so darn much golf,
It was outrageous, kiddo—
Fed up with that, I fear his wife
Was not a merry widow.

Walt Whitman

Walt Whitman always checked the wind
Before he made his pass—
In fact, he was the first one to
Rely on leaves of grass.

Charlie Chaplin

When Charlie Chaplin golfed, he walked;
No carts for him, praise be!
The reason was he didn't mind
A little tramp, you see.

Peter The Great

No one would play with Peter the Great,
A snub that he found crushin'—
Golf ought to be quite leisurely
And he was always Russian.

The Pied Piper

To play with the Pied Piper was
A bitter pill to swallow
'Cause, if he knocked it in a pond,
The rest knew they would follow.

Captain Kidd

The famous pirate Captain Kidd
With golf rules could not cope,
And therefore they suspended him—
In his case, from a rope.

Henry The Eighth

About this king I'd have to say
Golf was a game he dreaded—
He'd swing but never knew which way
His golf ball would beheaded.

Enrico Caruso

Caruso never golfed at all,
The game just didn't please—
He much preferred to sail and spent
His time on the high C's.

Robert Frost

Slow play was good for Robert Frost;
He didn't walk, he crept—
He did so knowing he had miles
To go before he slept.

Joan of Arc

Poor Joan of Arc, though way behind
In her match, had desire—
She went for bust but it was just
Too late when she caught fire.

Santa Claus

How good is Santa on the course?
By this you'll be uplifted:
He carries his own bag–what's more
Of course Saint Nick is gifted.

Madame Tussaud

When Madame Tussaud took up golf,
Her shanked shots made her spastic,
But later on, once those were gone,
She waxed enthusiastic.

John Milton

At times John Milton played quite well,
Won trophies, all embossed,
But when his smooth swing went to hell,
His paradise was lost.

The Hunchback of Notre Dame

No one thought Quasimodo was,
At golf, a real humdinger–
But they were wrong 'cause we know he
Quite clearly was a ringer.

Betsy Ross

Not once did Betsy Ross require
The kind of putt called lag—
There simply was no need since she
Was right next to the flag.

P.T. Barnum

The golf that P.T. Barnum played
Brought darn few compliments,
But, oh how he could concentrate!
No one was more in tents.

Arthur Murray

I know why Arthur Murray was
A stranger to golf's charms:
It's very hard to swing when you
Have someone in your arms.

Sherlock Holmes

The great detective Sherlock Holmes
Played golf but was a bomb—
He called for help from Watson but
His Watson wasn't Tom.

Stradivarius

It may be Stradivarius
Played golf and maybe not—
He probably was too high strung,
Which made him fret a lot.

Rip Van Winkle

Disqualified on the first tee
Was Rip Van Winkle's fate—
The starter ruled, alas, that he
Was twenty years too late.

Escoffier

The chef Escoffier did not
Think walking hills was smart—
And that is why, when this chef golfed,
He did it a la cart.

Lady MacBeth

The lady named MacBeth played once
And when, such was her lot,
A dog picked up her ball and ran,
She hollered "Out, damned Spot!"

D'Artagnan

D'Artagnan played golf lousily
And lost to all his peers—
He hung his head, but you could see
At least three musket tears.

Samson

Strong Samson hit the ball too far
And also couldn't putt—
That left it to Delilah who,
As we know, made the cut.

William Tell

No one asked William Tell to play,
Although he was no boor—
Apparently they all thought he
Would make the overture.

Martin Luther

Poor Martin Luther played at dusk,
Then tried to post his score—
The pro shop, though, was closed, so he
Just nailed it to the door.

Thomas Edison

The reason Thomas Edison
Played rotten golf, no doubt
Was that he simply couldn't bring
Himself to shoot lights out.

Whistler

The slightest sound upset this guy;
On greens he was a bristler;
He never played with family—
His mother was a Whistler.

Ginger Rogers

When Ginger Rogers played the game,
Her swing was only fair—
But I confess that nonetheless,
It left the guys Astaire.

Romeo and Juliet

Fair Juliet smiled down one night,
Her lover's heart to win—
Then Romeo made his pitch to
An elevated grin.

Peter Pan

When Peter Pan hit chip shots, their
Trajectory was grand—
They flew so high, you thought perhaps
They'd Never-Never land.

Count Dracula

Count Dracula despised our game,
Although he was no dud—
He couldn't stand to halve a hole
Because it meant no blood.

Edmund Halley

When Halley the astronomer,
Played golf, it made you vomit—
The guy was always looking up
And couldn't over comet.

Venus De Milo

The Venus named de Milo is
Admired in all the seasons,
But Venus doesn't play our game—
For pretty darn good reasons.

Julius Caesar

Greenkeepers back in ancient Rome
Had a complaint quite valid:
When Caesar found fault with their greens,
He put them on his salad.

Lady Godiva

The lady named Godiva could
Not always strike it squarely—
Small wonder then that those times when
She won, she did so barely.

Eli Whitney

Young Eli Whitney's pals played golf,
But he refused to do it—
And yet we see, from history,
He later cottoned to it.

John Philip Sousa

John Philip Sousa's game was poor
When heat made fairways parch;
But in the Spring he felt secure—
The man was great in March!

Helen of Troy

When this fair damsel took the tee,
Opponents quickly found
That she meant business instantly
And wooden horse around.

George M. Cohan

When George M. Cohan struck a shot,
It might go anywhere—
He aimed it for the grand old flag,
But it went Over There.

Glenn Miller

Glen Miller might have golfed more, but
His schedule would intrude;
And somehow, when he had the time,
He wasn't in the mood.

Johannes Gutenberg

That Gutenberg bet on his game
Is really not a guess,
For after all, as you'll recall,
The guy gave us the press.

Alexander Graham Bell

If Alexander Graham Bell
Played golf in his existence,
I'll make one guess about his game:
I'll bet he got long distance.

Florence Nightingale

I hear that Florence Nightingale
Was lousy with the sticks—
Her normal score, I've been advised,
Was ninety-eight point six.

Gulliver

Did Gulliver best everyone
Who teed up and defied him?
He did–until the day when all
The Lilliputians tied him.

Noah

Whenever Noah teed it up,
He really made his mark—
His drives were just tremendous 'cause
He had a bigger Ark.

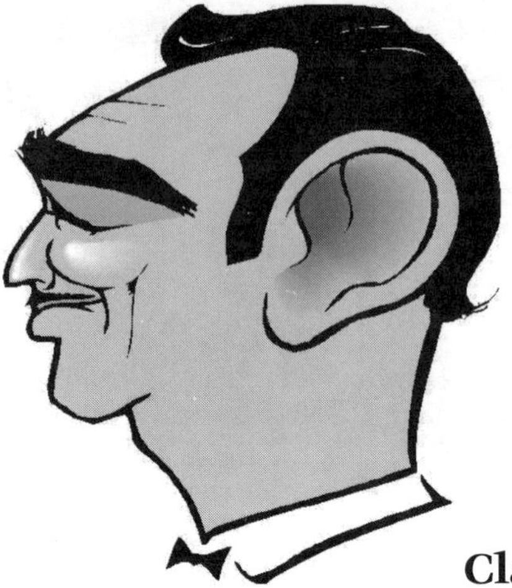

Clark Gable

Clark Gable could have been a pro
And might have won the Slam,
Excepting that, as we all know,
He didn't give a damn.

Robin Hood

The friar bested Robin Hood
At golf, thanks to some luck;
He had one putt on every hole–
Yep, that's all Friar Tuck.

Christopher Columbus

As golfers go, Columbus was
The worst to come in view—
The only score he's noted for
Was 1492.

Home Groan

Home Alone

Please etch this on my tombstone when
My body's cold and numb:
"This life was spent in waiting for
Some serviceman to come."

Home Groans

This tops my irritation list
And cuts, just like a knife can:
I can't find things around our house,
But, having failed, my wife can.

Searching Question

When household items need repair,
Breathes there a he and she
So organized that they know where
They put the warranty?

Miter Matter

The tools my neighbor owns have filled
His basement, wall to wall—
Is there some instrument he lacks?
Nope. This guy has them awl.

Inside Information

In our house we have many keys;
Some fit those doors and some fit these;
What worries me is that we've scores
Of keys for which we have no doors.

Closet Question

Around our house, coat hangers breed,
Each day their numbers swell—
Why is it they can do it here
But not in a motel?

Permanent Addition

Our bathroom has, besides the ones
Connected to the water,
A fixture others may not boast—
A fifteen-year-old daughter.

Sound Effect

I like to start a nice log fire
When winter storms are lurking—
And, every time I do, it proves
Our smoke detector's working.

Parcheesi Perhaps?

We now have three sets for TV,
Plus we tape shows on video—
Before all this stuff came to be,
I wonder what we dideo?

Tube Trauma

When TV game shows come in view,
I turn them off quite coolly;
I will not watch contestants who
Are smarter than Yours Truly.

Site Plight

Whenever there's a heavy snow,
Few persons are forlorner—
I'm twice as sad as most I know,
For I live on a corner.

Surface Reflection

Dogs with big tails and little kids
Are ready, willing, able
To make you wish you had removed
Things from your coffee table.

Double Delight

It is a joy to great our guests
Just as the party's starting;
An even greater bliss is this:
To see them all departing.

Perplexing Paradox

Most women do the cooking, but
What I have found bewitchin'
Is that, at every party, men
Will gather in the kitchen.

Picture Problem

All future photographs we take
We ought to file in drawers;
It's either that or buy six more
Refrigerator doors.

Tube Trauma

At six o'clock I watch the news;
I'm in despair by seven,
But it gets even worse when film
Is added at eleven!

Postal Probability

I often rail against junk mail,
That is, 'til I recall
That if I fail to get junk mail,
I won't get mail at all.

Hangers-On

You reach into a closet for
A hanger and most studies
Reveal that it will come out with
About six of its buddies.

Inside Information

With windows barred, lights in the yard
And deadbolts that can't fail,
There's still no place like home, but now
It looks a lot like jail.

Surface Reflection

Each time I hope for something good
And get enthusiastic
I look around to knock on wood,
But all I see is plastic.

Fitting Remark

The mink coat in the window caught
My helpmate's eager eyes;
The price was way beyond us, but
She tried it on for sighs.

Near Perfection

This ideal child of three or four
Deposits no clothes on the floor;
He doesn't think his toys a bore,
He loves them all and wants no more;
He never begs when in a store,
Sees Sunday School as fun galore;
He eats all veggies by the score
And with his sitter has rapport;
Who is this child I'm cheering for?
Why, he's the kid who lives next door!

Sound Defect

Is there a television ad,
(If so, I would adore it),
That isn't at least twice as loud
As what was on before it?

Marriage Matters

Shop Talk

At every big department store
Our credit's less than stellar—
I dread to tell my wife, therefore
I'll just let Bonwit Teller.

Lid Lines

As husbands go, I'm not the best
With whom you'll ever meet up—
My wife adores me, though, 'cause I
Don't leave the toilet seat up.

Medicine Jest

My wife's stuff fills the bathroom shelves;
Her guilty smile is elfish;
My lack of space prompts me to face
The fact my wife is shelfish

Gem Jam

When you buy earrings for your wife,
Dear fellow, you will find it
Quite likely that a matching pin
And ring are right behind it.

Color Scream

My wife set up a hue and cry
To paint the living room;
(I've acted on her hues and cries
Since when I was a groom).

I worked with might and also main,
And, once the paint had dried,
I brought her in the room, where she
Looked at the hue and cried.

Cold Fact

This message is for newlyweds
And even ardent daters:
A marriage, if it's good, will last
Through three refrigerators.

Task Mistress

My wife makes lists of chores for me
To do on days it rains;
Without her lists, she fears that I'll
Be listless, she explains.

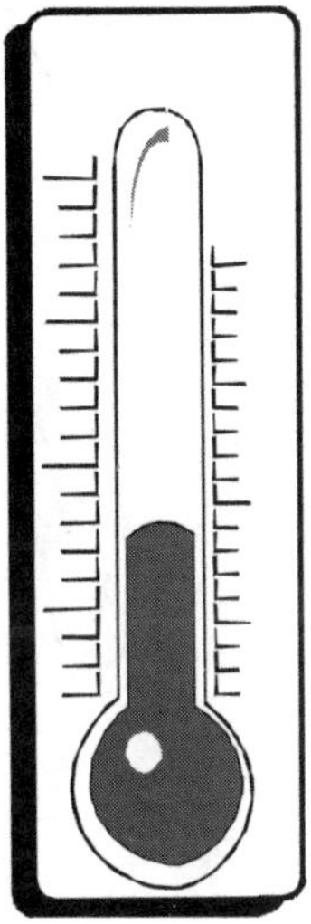

Degree Decree

We'd have far fewer household spats
If we abolished thermostats.

Cover Story

The carpet in our house displays
A vivid record of our days;
That strip of bareness, I think maybe
Is where we used to walk the baby;
A spike-heeled shoe produced that tear—
She held her post-prom party there!
The drink stains over which we grieve
Are echoes of some New Year's Eve;
A splotch that makes us even madder
Recalls our Spot and his weak bladder;
A family reunion made
Another mark that will not fade:
A little throw rug nicely cloaks
The burn by uncle Al, who smokes;
Why don't we just replace the thing?
We talk about it every Spring,
And every Spring the idea bores us—
Lose memories? The prospect floors us!

Reward of Restraint

My wife and I know married bliss,
Year in, year out we nuzzle;
Our love won't die—as long as I
Don't work her crossword puzzle.

The Right Stuff

Dear fellow husbands, here's advice
To make your marriage stronger:
If she admits that she was wrong
Insist that you were wronger.

Deciding Factor

In choosing her dress for a party,
My wife is bold and daring—
After she's sure (by telephone tour)
What Gladys, June, Frances, Charlotte,
Dottie, Phyllis, Mabel, Doborah, Mary
and Gertrude are wearing.

Clothed Subject

Each morning I select my tie,
Each morning it's a beaut!
Each morning my wife tells me that
It's all wrong for my suit.

Plate Mates

If one spouse washes dishes and
The other dries, I think
It works out rather well because
They're never out of sink.

Departing Lines

Each morning kiss your wife good-bye,
You harried, hurried cuss!
It's quite all right to miss the train
But *never* miss the buss!

Parallel Prescription

To keep your marriage and your teeth
In good health in your house,
Please squeeze the toothpaste twice a day—
Do likewise with your spouse.

Capital Idea

Financial stress can make a mess
Of marriage at its start—
Most couples now repeat this vow:
'Until debt do us part.'

Two Down

A marriage is in jeopardy
And looking down the muzzle
When *both* the partners want to work
The paper's crossword puzzle.

Growing Pains

"You're just a couch potato," said
My wife, at which I pouted;
I heatedly denied it, but
The other day I sprouted.

Bad Riddance

Each Spring my wife goes through her clothes
To toss what's antiquated—
But, when she's done, I note, not one
Thing's been eliminated.

It's a Given

My wife adores each gift of mine!
I've never seen her spurn it;
I'm filled with pride, aware inside
Tomorrow she'll return it.

Laundry Hampered

My wife was out of town a week
And made, of me, a liar—
I told her any fool can run
A washer and a dryer.

Negative Reaction

My wife is incoherent,
She's come apart in toto—
Her driver's license has arrived
And she has seen her photo.

Knot Note

The neckties I receive each Yule
From aunt or child or bride
All share one trait, I'm here to state—
They're not fit to be tied.

Crewel Thought

Her needlepoint lies here, lies there;
It clutters up the joint—
But, since it gives her joy, I guess
That is a petty point.

Byte Fright

There's no computer in our home
By order of my spouse;
I never should have told her that
They all come with a mouse.

Decks Appeal

Some think that solitaire is boring
And rank it right up there with snoring;
Why not, they ask, read books instead?
Or hear a tape or make some bread?
Don't sit there trying to determine
If you'll turn up a queen—learn German!
Go out, they urge, and breathe God's air—
Forget your double solitaire!
Does all this criticism ruffle?
You get the cards, my love, I'll shuffle.

Marriage Matter

Our daughter has been wed ten years,
A fact that pride instills,
And, in another ten, I'll have
Paid off the wedding bills.

Conjugal Conflict

This bride and groom were wed last week,
But now they will not nuzzle;
They just found out that each one wants
The daily crossword puzzle.

Return Report

We went back to Niagara,
Our troth vows to renew;
We saw the falls again -- it was
A case of deja view.

Vows View

She wed me for richer or poorer and,
Although it is distressful,
I'd have to say, as of today,
She's been halfway successful.

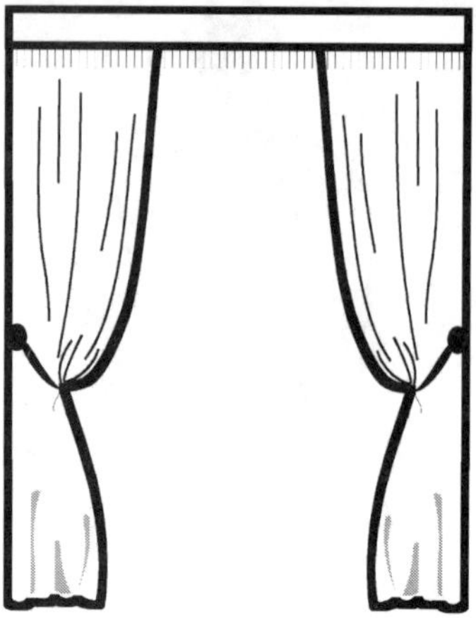

Furniture Fact

Through married life, there's been one truth
That I've found hard to swallow:
When we replace a lamp or chair,
New drapes are sure to follow.

Opposite Opinions

You couldn't keep me from the polls,
Not even with a mallet!
Hell or high water, I'll be there--
To cancel my wife's ballot!

Lotus Lines

When my wife does her yoga thing,
Contentment fills her cup;
She feels sublime -- as long as I'm
Around to help her up.

Favored Phrase

Three little words can cause my wife
To jump with joy and shout;
The magic words aren't "I love you" --
Instead, they're "Let's eat out!"

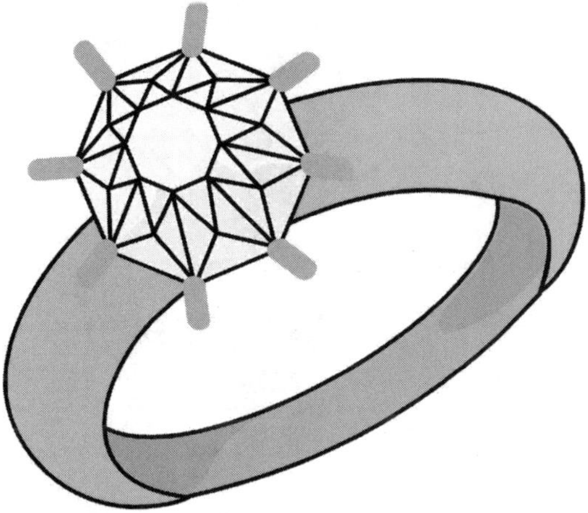

Gem Femme

One food that's very good for us,
We're often told, is carrots;
My wife agrees with that, but you
Should know she spells it karats.

Shared Similarities

The game of golf and marriages
Have many common parts;
For instance, both have rough spots and,
Quite often, shotgun starts.

Storage Squawk

This question has vexed married men
Since time was first begun:
Home come, with six-drawer chiffoniers,
The husband gets just one?

Control Confession

Our channel-changer's always in
My dear wife's hand, I note;
Some night I'd like to hold it, but
My chances are remote.

Golf Groan

Our marriage, which I thought was strong,
Has gone down hill on casters;
I just found out my wife has sold
My ticket to the Master's!

Dental Desire

Know what would make our marriage great?
To wake up some sweet dawn
And find, just once, that she has put
The toothpaste cap back on.

Carrying Case

Some new research has come to light
And now it's been disclosed
That women are much stronger than
Was heretofore supposed.

Here's my reaction to this news,
(And you'll call me a lout),
But, if this claim is true, why don't
They take the garbage out.

Money Maladies

Dollar Sighs

I don't have dough stashed in Swiss banks,
And while that is a pity,
What's worse is that the same is true
Of banks in my home city.

Bare Fact

Our kids are both in college now,
But here's what makes us blue:
Not only have they left the nest,
They took the nestegg, too.

Double Desire

There are two things this nation needs:
One is some brand-new heroes,
The other is a debt without
So gosh darn many zeroes.

Soybean Strategy

I don't trade in commodities,
Not for one blessed minute;
The reason is that I don't think
There's any future in it.

Certainty Surrender

Both death and taxes, it appears,
Are absolutely sure,
And I don't think for either one
We'll ever find a cure.

Buy Lines

The dictionary says "boutique"
Means shops both small and quaint;
The shops might be quite tiny, but,
Alas, the prices ain't.

Abbreviated Admission

I'm envious of those who hold
The stock known as pfd.—
I thought about some once, but my
Decision I dfd.

Income Outcome

I try each month to save some dough
For taxes, which are heavy;
Just like the song of long ago,
I'm working on the levy.

Meat Matter

I hate all creditors who pound
My door—may they be cursed!
The butcher frequently comes 'round
And I hate his knock worst.

Shrub Secret

Against inflation I've one hedge
That soaring costs can't batter;
I could reveal my hedge, of course,
But it's a privet matter.

Dow Discipline

The pilgrims were, I now concur,
As clever as a fox—
When someone bent the rules, they went
And put him into stocks.

Early Exit

Financial news was grim that day,
And here is what the shock did:
I up and panicked, sad to say,
And split before my stock did.

Form Feeling

They've changed the rules on income tax,
A fact that makes me burn—
I think perhaps that I have reached
The point of no return.

Window Pain

I wish my bank would hire a Bret,
A Nancy or Louise—
The tellers that I seem to get
Are named "Next Window Please."

Only a Memento

I have the first buck that I earned,
For which I'm envied, I've discerned;
But those who envy will be cheered
To know the rest have disappeared.

Hem Lines

The Dow goes up, the Dow goes down,
It helps you then it hurts;
It is almost as fickle as
The length of women's skirts.

Farewell Funds

My liquid assets, let me state,
Don't take long to evaporate.

Coming Clean

To "launder" money is a crime
And, what is more, me thinks,
There is no need to launder mine --
All by itself it shrinks.

Food Failure

Since I'm a couch potato now,
I won't, one clearly sees,
Become a top banana and
The same for a big cheese.

Artistic Anecdotes

Tympanist Terror

The symphony lulled me to sleep;
I dozed beside my wife;
Then cymbals crashed and I have not
Been scherzo in my life!

Sound Advice

To hear Puccini I will flock
And Verdi can't be missed—
But Wagner, Beethoven and Bach
Will never make my Liszt.

Exit Smiling

Most symphonies have movements that
Occur throughout the score;
Which movement do I like the best?
My movement toward the door.

Melody Mystery

This song has caused me sleepless nights
While rattling 'round my dome:
Won't someone kindly tell me if
Bill Bailey DID come home?

Sound Solution

When someone in a marching band,
A trombone, sax, or flute,
Goes to sick bay, quite calmly they
Insert a substitoot.

Sound Effect

The orchestra was terrible,
I do not mind confidin'—
The maestro threw down his baton
And then went into Haydn.

Notes Note

The cost of music lessons for
Our kids brought fiscal tears,
But they've all quit by now — and that
Is music to our ears.

Classic Answer

What's better, on a winter night
When snow the windows flock,
Than to put on a CD and
Curl up with a good Bach?

Violent Reaction

With movies they're showing,
I now take this tack;
I go out for popcorn
And never come back.

Pronoun Probability

Film-makers hurt the language so,
I won't be shocked to see,
If they do a revival, it
Will be "The King and Me".

View Point

The violence on movie screens
For youngsters isn't good;
YOU wouldn't want your kids to see
That stuff, but Hollywood.

Screen Test

When we decide to see a film,
With doubts we are not cluttered—
Forget the fare, we just go where
The popcorn will be buttered.

The Marriage of Figaro Has Almost Ended Ours

My wife thinks opera's exquisite;
Shanghaied, I'll make a yearly visit;
She loves sopranos, tenors, bassos
And gets me there by using lassoes;
While she's entranced by some great aria,
I fight—and lose—the language baria;
Boheme's last act will leave her cryin'—
(My taste runs more to Nolan Ryan);
Of operas, one thing is certain:
We both have feelings for the curtain;
When it goes up, her breathing stops—
I get excited when it drops.

Hot Doggerel!

Lord Byron saw his writings cease
When he got sick and died in Greece;
And Percy Shelley, though renowned,
Went for a sail and promptly drowned;
John Keats penned poetry that sticks,
But John Keats died at twenty-six.
In view of the forgoing curses,
I'm glad I just write silly verses.

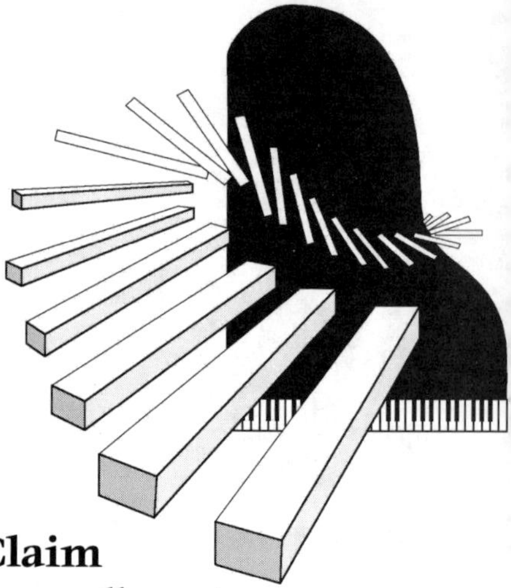

Classical Claim

Were the composers we call great
Immune to maidens' lures?
I do not see how that can be—
They all made overtures.

Seasonal Rhymes

Wet Warning

Old Winter's snow that yesterday
Was up above your arch
Will soon be water, so I say
Beware the tides of March!

Curb Disservice

In wintertime, pedestrians
Get splashed by car or truck—
I hope you've made it through unsprayed,
But I've had no slush luck.

Foot Note

Spring brings a flood of oozing mud
That soils your epiderma;
Of Spring's wet fare, please take my share—
I like my terra firma.

Soil of Approval

Small, solemn boys
To Spring relate—
They go outdoors and muditate.

The Goblins Raised Hob

I'd like to put light years between
Me and another Halloween;
This year I suffered ghoulish feats
'Cause I forgot to buy some treats.
On learning of my cupboard bare,
All hell filled the October air;
Some kid and my doormat eloped;
I own no pane that went unsoaped;
Porch chairs on which I take my ease
Decided to live in the trees;
The backyard fence I so adored
Evaporated, board by board;
Because I goofed and lacked confections,
My roof antenna's now in sections;
Next year will matters be improving?
I guess I'll never know. I'm moving.

Christmas Question

December means decision time
Sufficient to upset one:
Do we send cards to those from whom
Last year we didn't get one?

Precipitous Decision

I hate the winter, goodness knows;
(Cold weather makes me achey);
But there are those who love the snows—
It's obvious they're flaky.

Season Treason

Where are the joys of Summer?
Where is the Loop-the-Loop?
The swimming, golfing, sailing?
All gone in one Fall swoop.

Autumn Admiration

I hate to see the Summer leave
And yet (don't think me odd)
Fall's colors are so lovely, they
Must be an Oct. of God.

One is Fun

That Christmas comes but once a year
I cannot disagree
But, what with fees for gifts and trees,
Once is enough for me.

Seasonal Suggestion

Dear helpmate, when you Christmas shop
This year, don't go insane, dear;
I beg, implore, when in the store,
Don't fail to use the rein, dear.

Position Statement

When there is mistletoe on high
Above a girl who's very shy,
Although she sees what has been planned,
It's hard for her to under stand.

Displeasin' Season

Some people sing your praises, Spring,
Exulting at each bud;
But you're too wet to be my pet—
To me, your name is mud.

Foot Note

In Spring, our tyke strolls off to school
To get some knowledge pumped in—
And he makes sure that, on his tour,
No puddle goes unjumped in.

Christmas Is When We Don't Have Much Card Sense

Our Christmas cards have all been written
And, in the doing, I've been smitten
By the thought that somehow we
Are sending them exclusively
To people whom we really shouldn't,
And I, for one, wish that we wouldn't.
The reason for my seeming mutiny
Is that our list, when given scrutiny,
Reveals that we are sending cards
To folks who own adjacent yards;
To those who've moved to Neb. or Tenn.
And whom we'll never see again;
To those with whom I work each day
As if, somehow, I were away.
But worse than sending cards to these
Is that each Christmastime we seize
The chance to send Noelatives
To all our diverse relatives,
Who, barring strike or crippling storm
(And if things happen true to form),
Will Christmas Day be gaily sittin' at
The very board their cards were written at.

Cover Story

We save Yule wrappings every year,
The ribbons, too, that bind them;
We even save the bows, but then
The next year we can't find them.

Early Entrance

To Spring's first robin
I say, "Hello"—
So sorry about
The foot of snow.

Let's Face it, February!

Most years you rate just twenty-eight,
While other months they stuff—
And, while you may decry your fate,
In *your* month, that's enough!

Unique Unit

That summer is so popular
Seems strange when you recall
It is the only season that
Is heading for a fall.

Pine Lines

Each Yule we buy a nice new tree
And set it up indoors to see;
For days on end, while corn is popping,
We listen to the needles dropping;
How come we slash the forest firs
And bring them in? A thought occurs:
(I will explain 'cause I know how to)—
It's a tradition that we bough to.

Concealment Conclusion

In Wintertime, when women wear
High boots, let me disclose,
They do so just to cover up
Runs in their pantyhose.

Cold Fact

By the time he's suited
And scarved and booted
And mittened and capped
And zippered and snapped
And tucked and belted—
The snow has melted.

Everything's Relative

Thanksgiving Day is when I'm with
A ton of kin and also kith;
One time of year our clan will gather—
Some hate to be there, some would rather;
Foredoomed, I share sweetmeats and wassails
With folks I thought by now were fossils;
My interest is somewhat forced
In learning who from whom divorced;
To dandle babies I'm not strong to
When I'm not sure whom they belong to;
If this year's ends in hugs and kissin',
Next year they'll find Yours Truly missin'.

Go Away Groundhog!

When February 2 comes, sports,
I never read the news reports
To find out if the groundhog's spied
His shadow in the countryside;
It matters not what groundhogs say
'Cause where I live and taxes pay,
Six added weeks of snow and storm
Is, I regret to say, the norm.

This Creature Is Not Stirring

Dear helpmate, let's get one thing clear:
I will not play St. Nick this year;
No pillows at the waist, no whiskers,
No jumps from roofs or other riskers;
Last year when I dressed like St. Nicholas,
The neighbors said I looked ridicholas;
I will not be the Jolly Elf,
I'd rather be my surly self;
You can't coerce me, love, because
Our contract has no Santa clause.

Mail Wail

Friends' Christmas letters to us fly;
We get them by the dozen;
They gag us with achievements by
Each kid, each spouse, each cousin.

Of boastful missives this I shrill:
If you feel you *must* breed them,
Please be advised the chance is nil
That I will ever read them.

Fall's Alarm

No thought I know of leaves me number
Than that we're nearly through with summer;
The longish evenings, filled with peace,
Will, now that autumn's on us, cease;
Before we know it every night'll
Be wrecked by a ballet recital,
A meeting of the PTA
Or else the fourth grade's yearly play;
And if, by chance, one evening's clear,
The bridge club will be playing—here;
I would that August could be kept
And never, ever become Sept.

View Point

A lighted Christmas tree looks nice;
Without my lenses, though, it's twice
As beautiful! It then becomes
A garden of chrysanthemums!
I'd rather not be near of sight
Except on Christmas Eve or night;
That's when it's fairyland, Utopia!
I'm sorry you can't share myopia.

Liquor Lines

When I go out on New Year's Eve,
I drink to get a buzz
And hope that I don't drop before
The ball in Times Square does.

Northern Note

It's March and the first robin's back,
A sight that's very pleasing;
It's clear he leads the robin pack—
It's also clear he's freezing.

Next Question

If Winter comes, as Shelley asks,
Can Spring be far behind?
As luck would have it where *I* live,
The answer's yes, I find.

Time Rhyme

In Spring, you should re-set your clocks;
If I forget or stall,
I never fret or break a sweat —
I'll be okay come Fall.

Sports

Golf Grimace

The 'gator on the course and I
Felt hatred for each other;
I loathe the thing—and he could see
My shoes were once his mother.

Pre-Season Proposal

Dear baseball team, the world agrees
You'll finish fifth or fourth—
If that's a fair assessment, please
Don't bother coming north.

Ache Annoyance

I've tennis elbow, swimmer's ear,
My athlete's foot's pathetic—
What makes my suffering severe
Is that I'm not athletic.

Matter of Degree

Those college gridders who know this
I have to praise as clever:
A pigskin is important, but
A sheepskin is forever.

Golf Grief

You say you're playing well, my friend?
You've dodged golf's ancient voodoo?
Well, just when things are looking up,
I'll bet a nickel you do!

Sound Reasoning

Home-crowd support in any sport
With glee makes coaches dance;
It helps a lot, but you cannot
Leave everything to chants.

Golf in Granite

If you should read my tombstone, friend,
Here's what would meet your eye:
It isn't dying I resent,
It's this damn buried lie!

Holy Uncalled For

This quarterback's decision was,
To say the least, distressing—
He threw a long "Hail Mary" pass
Without the coach's blessing.

Abnormal Athlete

In basketball, this guy's unique
And worthy of a cheer:
Though lured by pros, he stayed in school
Right through his freshman year!

Baseball Benefit

Your hotdog's cold, your beer is warm,
A post your view impairs—
Cheer up! Where else could you get close
To eighteen millionaires?

Shirt Tale

I couldn't make the varsity,
But once, avoiding eyes,
I snitched the jersey of a star
And tried it on for sighs.

Unlikely Utterance

Just once before this vale I quit
Or get too old and drowsy,
I'd like to hear some coach admit
His next opponent's lousy.

Preferred Package

I know why baseball earns the love
This nation has exuded:
It is the only game that comes
With batteries included.

Dessert Decision

Some football coaches go for cakes
And some for pies, no doubt—
But all agree, predictably,
That turnovers are out.

Golf Grimace

I do not have to be a sage
To know I'll never shoot my age,
But, what scares me, from toe to pate,
Is that someday I'll shoot my weight.

Mike Flight

Ballplayers who no longer hit
And cannot field the bouncers
Don't have to be alarmed one bit—
They'll turn into announcers.

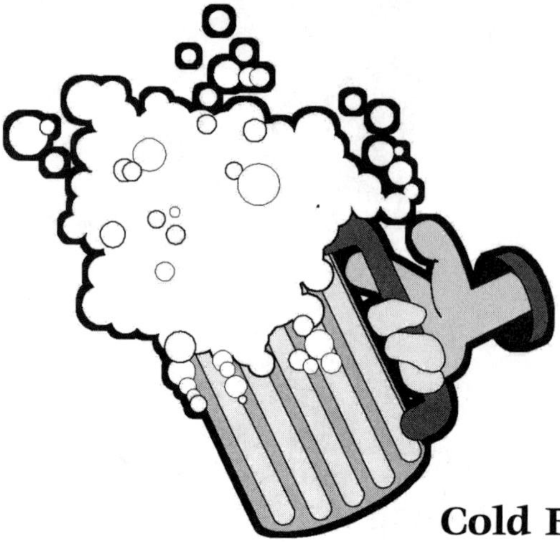

Cold Fact

Ice fishing on a lake is free
There isn't any ante;
Please help yourself to all that glee—
But, as for me, I shanty.

Brewhaha

There's so much beer at baseball games,
In bottles, cups and cans,
The bases don't get loaded half
As often as the fans.

Surface Reflection

Some football teams play on a rug,
A smooth, man-made creation;
Some play on grass before the mass
And some play on probation.

Game Pan

When TV spots a cute young thing,
They'll from the action veer—
Alas, a pretty girl is like
A malady, I fear.

Ring Ritual

He jabbed his man into the ropes
With lefts that were delights,
Then moved him to the center and
Delivered the last rights.

Despite Their Pleading

No lawyer can play tennis well,
And this is why, in short:
Most of their lob shots, truth to tell,
Will settle out of court.

Ice Inquiry

At times this skating pair's sublime,
At times they're just third-raters
And so I ask, from time to time,
How can you figure skaters?

Food Fraud

My first dog show was quite a bore,
Although I'm not demanding—
I only went because they swore
The chow would be outstanding.

Throw Threat

I used to run the mile in track,
But never was outstanding—
The one thing on my mind was where
The javelins were landing.

Holiday Hope

This grid team had gone 0 for 10,
The coach feared for his living—
Hard-pressed to win, the guy put in
The wishbone for Thanksgiving.

Lake Loss

The fish I hooked looked huge to me!
He must have been a daddy!
He wriggled free and was, you see,
The fin I almost haddie.

Smart Start

My horse broke cleanly from the gate!
His first few leaps were strong!
He took the lead, my noble steed—
But not, alas, furlong.

Snow Job

I've tried to learn to ski, but it's
The only sport, I'll bet,
In which, if you don't get the drift,
The drift is what you get.

Literary Logic

I don't know what ballplayers read,
(I'm not a clubhouse roamer),
But I must say, if I were they,
I'd concentrate on Homer.

Slope Hope

I'd feel at ease
When I'm on skis
If God would please
Remove His trees.

Ring Rap

When Hell has frozen over, chum,
When dogs with cats are nestling,
When marching bands don't have a drum,
That's when I'll watch Pro wrestling.

Links Label

My tombstone will read simply "PAR";
It's not a carving blunder;
For all these decades, par is what
I've wanted to be under.

Numeral Note

When early Romans played at golf
And hit bad shots galore,
No one got killed, no blood was spilled
Because they hollered IV!

Position Petition

I hope the cemetery's flat
When finally I die;
One thing I would not like is this:
Another downhill lie.

Pool Problem

In dives from the 10-meter board,
I'm nervous and I show it;
It's not the height so much as the
Three-meter board below it.

Relief Report

A bullpen pitcher never runs,
I think it's fair to mention;
He slowly strolls so he will be
The saunter of attention.

Foot Note

This golfer hung two stockings by
His chimney, which was done
So that St. Nick could verify
He had a hole in one!

Talking Point

A loser gets no interview
To tell us how he feels,
Which proves again, I guess, that to
The winners go the spiels.

Motion Notion

The third base coach goes through his signs
To hit or take or squeeze;
My wife, no baseball fan, opines:
"I think that man has fleas."

Plate Fate

This baseball player chased the skirts
Wherever he would roam;
He was so bad, his wife got mad
And threw him out at home.

Sad Situation

So many schools now break the rules
Where big-time football's played,
The goalposts are the only things
Still upright, I'm afraid.

Racquet Racket

The kid hit tennis balls against
His house until he cried;
His swing improved and, as it grooved,
His folks went deaf inside.

Is It Knot So?

I've never sailed and I'm aware
I've missed one of life's joys—
It must be fun to be out there
With all the gulls and buoys.

Direct Dejection

I'll never be a tennis star
Or even win my share;
The trouble is my placements are
Somewhat the worse for where.

Wheel Wail

In sports, golf tops the high cost list,
And that is true, in part,
Because most courses now insist
You play it a la cart.

Special Delivery

The way the seasons overlap,
A smile I would not crack
If I should see a knuckleball
Thrown to a nickel back.

Elevating Thought

This baseball manager is fit,
Not one ounce is unsightly;
How does he stay so muscled, pray?
By lifting pitchers nightly.

Pulpit Pitch

My minister's a baseball nut;
Instead of crime and sinning,
Week after week, he talks of how
It was in the big inning.

Fatherly Fear

There is one place in basketball
Where I don't want my kid
And that is on the top of a
Cheerleaders' pyramid.

Grid Groan

The price of tickets, parking and
The hotdogs that you get
Replace the pass, the kick, the run
As football's triple threat.

Night Nag

The track was bathed in sun that day,
Old Sol shone down like sin;
I bet the <u>dark</u> horse, which is when
The stupid thing came in.

Tennis Trauma

I cannot blame my racquet when
My play is less than deft;
I also cannot blame the balls—
There's only one thing left.

Golf Guilt

My Christmas tree this year will be
The nicest one you'll ever see!
Do you recall that lovely pine
That used to gather drives—all mine?
Well, call it theft or call it treason,
That pine will not be there next season!

Grid Groan

Now see the football stadia
Fill up with men and ladia,
Now see the halfback throw the pass
In trembling flight above the mass,
Now see the end receiver dart,
Now watch the goalward running start,
Now see the guy behind me rise
And smash my hat across my eyes.

I'm Not Blind Inclined

Duck hunters, do not try my door
When eager-eyed, at half-past four
You sally forth and try to take
A wild (but non-existent) drake;
I am, I fear, a disbeliever
In sitting down with some retriever
And holding, cramped and chilled and tired,
A shotgun that is never fired;
No, even though I risk affronting,
You hunt the ducks; I'll duck the hunting.

Diamond Desire

When baseball teams give caps to fans,
Someone's account grows fatter;
Quite candidly, I'd like to be
The Designated Hatter.

Parchment Problem

Now here's a verity in sport
That you can have and hold:
A team that's good on paper is
Quite likely, pal, to fold.

Florida Finding

I'm sure that 'gators eat golf balls
And proof I do not lack;
How else do you account for all
Those knobs upon his back?

Brave on Blades

Some skaters do a figure eight;
I can't do even seven,
But, knowing that I'm tempting fate,
I sometimes try eleven.

Sabbath Sin

Once I have played my Sunday golf,
It takes no deep research
To prove my minister was right—
I should have gone to church.

Links Law

In terms of golf here is a fact,
That can not be rebutted:
There is no green upon this earth,
That cannot be four-putted.

Cage Question

When watching basketball, my wife
Admittedly is lost;
She sees a <u>free</u> throw, then inquires
"What do the <u>others</u> cost?"

Travel Troubles

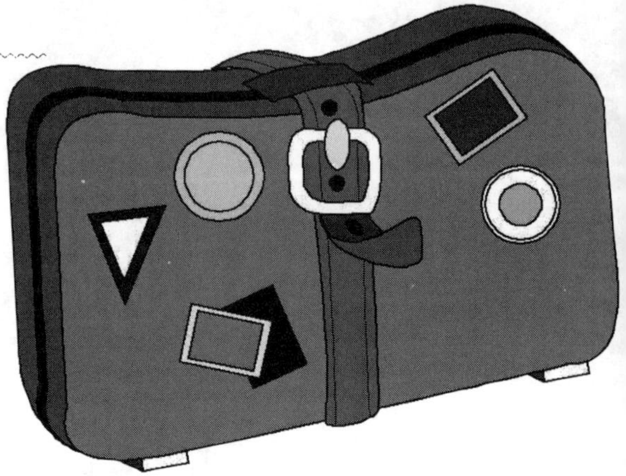

Air Lines

Why is it that it always takes
(I'd like a good reply here)
Far longer to retrieve my bag
Than it took me to fly here?

Duds Dilemma

We've learned a lot from traveling,
My wife and I together—
And mainly it's that what she's brought
Is all wrong for the weather.

It's Great, Britain!

I visit Shakespeare's area
At every chance I get
To taste the food that Romeo
And, doubtless, Juli et.

Bad Seine

When someone mentions Paris, I'm
Afraid I just stare blankly—
I'd really like to see it, but
I can't afford it, francly.

River Report

I went to London, saw the gems
And took a boat ride on the Thames;
When loudly I pronounced it "Thaymes,"
It broke up fifteen cricket games.

Screen Test

They've talked of their vacation trip,
Told front and back and sides of it—
And now, unless I miss my guess,
They're gonna show the slides of it.

Joy Ride

If getting there is half the fun,
The other half, God knows,
Is learning it's the same place where
The airline sent your clothes.

Boat Note

I took my wife to Venice once,
But, since then, we've stayed clear;
I'm pretty sure that, on our tour,
I saw the gondo leer.

Lost Cause

When asking for directions on
A trip, I'd think it's bliss
If someday I could find the spots
They said I couldn't miss.

Acceleration Admission

Speed limits now are on the rise,
Which scares me and here's why:
My auto shakes at seventy
And, frankly, so do I.

Galaxy Guess

Someday a flight to Mars will be
Part of our normal pattern—
Our luggage, almost certainly,
Will all be sent to Saturn.

Auto Suggestion

They're making "smarter" cars these days,
Thanks to Detroit's contrivers,
But let me say cars long have been
Much smarter than their drivers.

Color Scheme

When, in your car, you've loads of time
To get to some cotillion,
The traffic lights are green, but when
You're late, they're all vermillion.

Stern Warning

The threat on this "No Parking" sign
Has left me seeing stars:
"All violators will be towed—
So also will their cars."

Auto Anguish

My drive behind this motorist
I wouldn't call relaxing—
In one hand was his phone and with
The other he was faxing.

Noise Note

There's no such thing as a motel,
(A fact that makes me fume),
That doesn't have an interstate
Ten feet outside your room.

Affairs of States

1.
Nevada wants us to come out;
With glitzy ads they beg us—
But, as to notions why we go,
I do not have the Vegas.

2.
In Florida, the door's ajar
For winter's refugees,
And if, by error, it gets locked,
Don't fret. They've got the keys.

3.
The state of California calls
And to it I would waltz
Excepting that, from what I've seen,
It has some major faults.

4.
In Colorado, mountains are
The feature that's unique,
Especially the one called Pike—
That's surely worth a peek.

Paris May Not Be Burning, But I Am

In France, my helpmate bought perfume,
Enough to make their Dow-Jones zoom;
She also bought designer clothes,
(Designed to swell my fiscal woes);
More than the francs she spent like air,
Here's why I didn't think it fair:
I bought French postcards from some crook
At which I'm not allowed to look.

X Marks the Spa

Trips to the mountains or the beach
Financially are out of reach;
Although we'd love to look at Europe,
My wallet says to give that tour up;
San Fran is someplace we could shoot for;
But which we also lack the loot for;
Where *can* we go this coming year?
The answer, I'm afraid, is here.

Intersection Info

Fast-driving motorists, as through
The yellow lights they clamber,
Should know the lights, unlike the book,
Are not forever amber.

Trip Trauma

Our trip this year seemed to be cursed:
The air connections were the worst,
The sights weren't what they'd said at first,
The scheduled stage troupes had dispersed,
The guides were, at their best, unversed,
In day-long rains we were immersed,
We both caught colds (the which we nursed),
To just get home was our great thirst—
And, when we did, the pipes had burst.

Train Trend

Does there exist a town today
(An answer's what I want)
Whose railroad station has not yet
Become a restaurant?

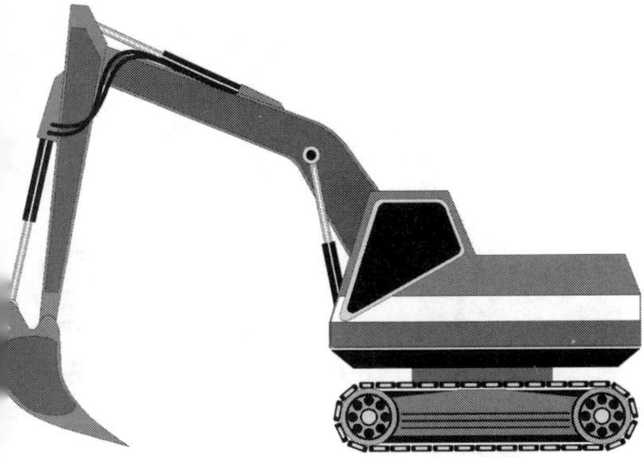

Road Rage

In summertime, the interstates
Of snow and ice are bare;
That coincides, of course, with when
They're torn up for repair.

On the Horn of a Dilema

The light turns green; the guy ahead
Seems to be half asleep;
As Hamlet did, I ask myself:
To beep or not to beep?

You're almost Great, Britain!

The English are a noble strain,
Despite the fact they live in rain;
They've got Big Ben, they've got the Thames,
And, in the tower, all those gems!
They've got their pubs, their cliffs of Dover,
They've got cathedrals, pal, all over!
To England, great regard I bring
Excepting for one little thing:
I wish—in fact I'm almost praying—
That I could fathom what they're saying.

Arresting Thought

The thoughtful motorist's no myth;
I'll tell you where to find him:
Look for the guy who's driving with
A cop car right behind him.

Miscellaneous Musings

Losing Cause

My supermarket's like a child
And proves it every week
By offering another game
Of hiding what I seek.

Door Jam

I very rarely lock my car,
(There isn't much to seize in it)—
And, on those few times when I do,
Of course I've left my keys in it.

Fang Fact

My dog won't bite a postman 'cause
I've trained him to be good,
But, based on what is in my mail,
I sometimes wish he would.

Fluid Fact

All babies are adorable
Except for one thing, friend:
When on your lap, they're very apt
To leak at either end.

Law Flaw

Now here's a truth that troubles me,
Indeed, leaves me unstrung:
A criminal can go scot-free
But juries can be hung.

Noun Note

When someone's grammar is so bad
It almost makes me faint,
Am I the kind who promptly will
Correct the guy? I ain't.

Night Note

Insomnia must be a chore
For those folks subject to it—
I don't believe I've had it, or,
If so, I slept right through it.

Cheers for Czechoslovakia!

Although that country has no flair
In terms of modern tech,
I take great joy in knowing they're
Still dancing Czech-to-Czech.

Rewarding Revelation

For ultimate bliss, I nominate this
(And all other pleasures I'm scorning):
To wake with a jerk, think you're tardy for work
And discover it's Saturday morning.

Forlorn Fact

Here is a truth that, man and boy,
I've spent a lifetime ruing:
There isn't much that I enjoy
I don't feel guilty doing.

Post Pest

I don't think of my college much,
In truth, it's almost never—
But, from my mail, it's clear that they'll
Remember me forever.

Inside Job

Note to the sore inside my mouth:
For you I have not hankered;
I wish you'd quit, but there you sit—
You came, you saw, you cankered.

Auto Biography

This tops the list of all the things
That do no earthly good:
When my car stalls, I hop right out
And look beneath the hood.

Snack Knack

Machines that vend enjoy, no end,
Their gift to bringing woe to you:
They're out of what you want and then
Will not return your dough to you.

Inside Information

Stalactites hang, Stalagmites rise
In caverns underground—
That much I know—or maybe it's
The other way around.

Seeing is Bereaving

Each night, before to sleep I've gone,
I pray the Lord in heaven
Will undo all I've witnessed on
The newscast at eleven.

Carton Custom

When I receive a package, I
Will fight it open, friend,
Then, as I quit, I'll read where it
Says "Open Other End."

Fish Wish

At cocktail gatherings, we strive,
With planning that is deft,
To time things so that we'll arrive
Before the shrimp have left.

Not the Tape Type

I count that day as really grand,
One truly fit for hoarding,
When I make several phone calls and
Do not get a recording.

Saline Solution

A low-salt diet is for me,
And, while I might complain of it,
I get my share because, you see,
I take things with a grain of it.

Sip Tip

Decaffeinated coffee is
The only kind I brew—
The reason is I'd like to stay
Decoffinated, too!

Alphabet Admission

When picking out a film, I must
Confess, quite naughtily,
The movies rated "X" are just
The ones I want to Z.

Royal Regret

No coat of arms adorns my door,
My bedstand, car or desk—
I'd like to be nobility,
But that's too much to esq.

Down Syndrome

All crossword puzzles authors use,
It is my observation,
An awful lot of words you don't
Hear in a conversation.

Container Complainer

Dear milk inside your cardboard box,
I love you and I'm hopin',
Before I go stark, raving mad,
That I will get you open.

Floor Plan

Our daughter is ecstatic,
But I'm a mental wreck—
For college, she's selected
A school named Disco Tech.

Outside Information

Dear Mother Nature, please know that
My auto is brand-new;
I'll keep it nice at any price—
The rust is up to you.

The Young Refrain

Time was when families were large,
I scarce knew one that wasn't;
But now young marrieds use restraint—
It's cheaper by the doesn't.

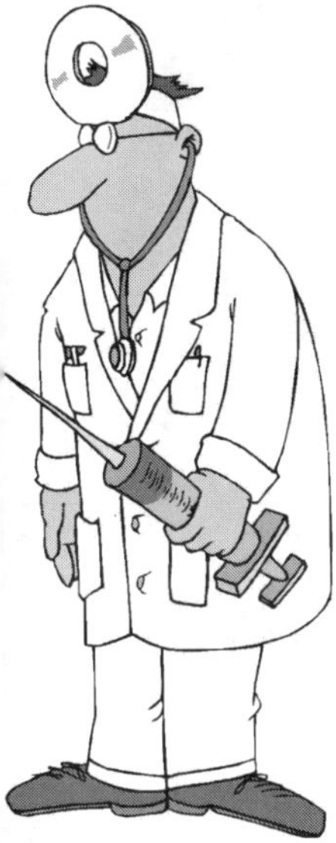

Medi-Sin

Physicians are so specialized,
You don't know where to go;
You hurt your foot, but when you call
They want to know which toe?

Language Lament

The pronouns known as personal
Confuse us, though we try;
Nobody seems to get them right,
Except, of course, for I.

Mail Moon

Nor Snow, nor rain, nor gloom of night,
Nor winter's cruel ices
Can stay the Postal Service from
Increasing its stamp prices.

Draft Notice

In hospitals, they poke and prod;
All privacy I lack
'Cause, in that gown that makes me frown,
My life's an open back.

Nightingale Note

Most nurses seem to love their work
And do it with a flair;
How is it nothing seems to irk?
It's their esprit de care.

Old Story

If one possesses great antiques
In each and every room,
(The kind that everybody seeks),
That's when an heir will loom.

Position Statement

The thing to do,
When you're in limbo,
Is simply stand there,
Arms akimbo.

Ironclad Memory

The Monitor and Merrimac
Were enemies, it's true—
But which was North and which was South?
I'm never sure. Are you?

Agrarian Admission

A city boy, I'll never spy
A field of things a-growing
The nomenclature of which I
Have any chance of knowing.

Don't point me towards a stand of beans
And order "Name that plot"
'Cause I will not know if those beans
Are soy or if they're not.

And, as for barleys, wheats and ryes,
I am an ignoramus—
The farmers laugh at urban guys
And plant those things to shame us.

There isn't one crop they can grow
That I can—surely—label;
Forgive me, farm friends, but please know
I want them on my table.

Speed Need

The preacher drones on endlessly,
The sermon's a disaster;
As I sit there, I fear my prayer
Is for a faster pastor.

Bone Belief

I hadn't thought of this before,
Although my years are numerous:
We label it the "funny bone"
'Cause part of it is humerus.

Tale of Whoa

A horse named Chaucer looked to be
The best—I wasn't worried;
But Chaucer merely *trotted* in
The stretch, his canter buried.

Missing Materials

Among the things I'll never see,
One is the Holy Grail—
Another is, it's clear to me,
The check that's in the mail.

Prodigy Presumption

Some infants show their genius when
They're young enough for bibbing;
I can't believe how smart they are—
I think they must be cribbing.

Bare Fact

Exotic dancers,
As one sees,
Possess a certain
Expertease.

Postal Pout

I curse the cost of stamps that on
My envelopes I'm sticking—
I moisten and apply them, but
It's I who takes the licking!

Gum Lines

Our kids have grown, so dental bills
Don't scare me as before—
I'm very glad I don't have to
Bicuspids any more.

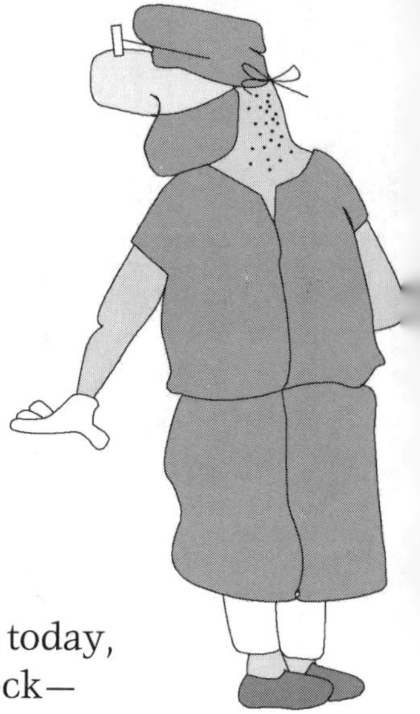

Ail Wail

Health costs are out of sight today,
Each new bill brings a shock—
They'll simply have to dock my pay
If I'm to pay my doc.

Commandments Confession

The Ten Commandments I have kept,
The large ones and the small of them;
I'm pretty sure I have—except
I can't remember all of them.

Poirot Pout

My cheeks are sunk, I'm in a funk;
My angry eyes are misty—
I found out I've read everything
There is by Agatha Christie.

Rank Idea

We need more heroes in this world;
The fact is unassailable—
And, as good luck would have it, friends,
It happens I'm available.

Departing Lines

Is there a graduate somewhere,
Brand-new or gray of head,
Who knows a single thing that his
Commencement speaker said?

Garment Gripe

Most dresses that the stores display
Are meant for ladies thin—
So who can wear these tiny things?
Only a mannequin.

Knight Note

Queen Guinevere was Arthur's wife,
Although she loved him not;
Oh, she stayed faithful all her life,
But she liked Lance a lot.

Word Wisdom

Who labels it the mother tongue?
Why, ten folks out of ten do;
It's known as that, dear ladies, 'cause
You use it more than men do.

Smile Suggestion

Next time you think you're gonna frown,
Please try to do it upside down.

Short Stewardship

Our youngsters often bring home strays
And care for them...the first two days.

Painful Prediction

The problem facing every wannabe
Is that, most likely, he's not gonnabe.

Lake Loss

When asked to name the five Great Lakes,
I feel somewhat inferior;
Oh, I can get Lake Michigan
And Huron and Superior;
Ontario's the fourth, of course,
But then my brain grows weary
And I can never name the fifth—
It's absolutely Erie!

Standing Order

You let a boy-child on your lap
And several things are bound to hap:
Your trousers' precious knife-like crease
Will, in a couple seconds, cease;
The youngster's ice cream becomes rivery
And promptly inundates your livery;
The glasses that you wear to see with
He bends and breaks, his little knee with;
The moral should be plain to spot,
But here it is, in case it's not:
When near a tyke who roams unchecked,
The wise man will remain erect.

Trouser Truth

By men's suspenders I'm depressed;
Suspendered men look half undressed;
They hold your pants up, but what else
Performs that task? Why, good old belts!
A belt provides the same suspension
Without demanding your attention;
Sure, go ahead and wear your galluses—
But they look dumb. That's my analluses.

Skin Supposition

A hunter stalking deer will try
To find him and outguess him;
With any luck, he'll shoot a buck
And then proceed to "dress" him.

But, from the viewpoint of the prey,
This thought one can't ignore:
He doubtless much preferred the way
That he was dressed before.

Vine Lines

The grads of Princeton, Harvard, Yale
Top most alumni giving
Because from their diplomas they
Have made a lovely living.
But there's another reason quite
Aside from their class rings:
They keep a strong attachment 'cause
It's true that ivy clings.

Earth Exit

The reason no one's ever seen
A Martian's clear to me:
They land, then leave abruptly 'cause
They don't like that they see.

Germ Journal

A swift little virus named Enza
Peered in as I waxed my credenza;
I threw open a pane,
became drenched by the rain,
And, quick as a flash, in flew Enza.

Dead Reckoning

Morticians hold conventions, too,
And make the normal whoop-de-doo;
They laugh and joke and sing and all
And no one there is bearing pall;
Their glee I've tried hard to assess--
It's their esprit de corpse, I guess.

Let's Face It

The ads claim that this after shave
Will bring girls to your side;
I douse my face with it each morn
And, you know what? They lied.

Office Ode

Most people own computers, but
I haven't bought one yet;
If you intend to reach me, friend,
Please use the Outernet.

Nature Note

We're killing the environment;
Here's proof and you can't block it:
How long since you've seen a boy with
A frog inside his pocket?

Reprise Report

I had a very misspent youth
With smokes and girls and gin;
If I could just relive it, I'd
Misspend it all again.

Surface Reflection

Incessantly we search for oil,
Then, once it's found, we drill it
And put it in a tanker which
Will then proceed to spill it.

Response Report

If I should face a firing squad
And questioned, I will answer
"Yes, I would like one final smoke—
I'd rather die of cancer."

Mixed Message

No bumper stickers on your car?
That either means you're clever
Or else that somehow you have no
Opinions whatsoever.

Safe Salutation

I can't remember peoples' names,
No, not for love or money;
That's largely why each evening I
Greet my wife with "Hi, honey!"

Contagious Captivity

You sit in doctors' waiting rooms
'Til boredom you get numb with;
What's worse, you're there so long you catch
What someone else has come with.

Rail Report

If you can't finish some remark,
I think you can deduce
You lost your train of thought before
You got to the caboose.

Preferred Position

I often find,
Once I have dined,
I have a mind
To be reclined.

Gift of Grab

When pickpockets retire, do they
Their life's work then abandon?
My guess is no because a pro
Would want to keep his hand in.

Lines for a Would-Be Lover

A dozen roses win the girl;
If she has doubts, they'll free it;
A nice perfume might work, but three
Martinis guarantee it.

Hair Lines

If being bald is beautiful,
As bald men like to say,
Then I am getting prettier
With every passing day.

Birth Defect

Some folks seem surly all life long;
They dish scowls with a ladle;
I must presume they got out of
The wrong side of the cradle.

Penmanship Puzzle

If doctors are so gosh darn smart,
As everybody claims,
Will someone kindly tell me why
They cannot write their names?

Talking Point

To gossip is an evil thing,
Revealing a mean spirit,
But, if you have to gossip, please
Do it so I can hear it.

Removal Report

If you research your family tree
Of long-dead hers and hims,
The chances are you'll find you'd like
To saw off several limbs.

Scripture Revisited

The meek, because of all their merit,
Will, it is writ, the world inherit;
That's gospel and I do not taunt it—
But I'm not sure the meek will want it.

Brave Bunch

It's claimed we have no heroes, but
That talk makes me see red;
Aren't we forgetting those folks who
Are teaching driver's ed?

Word Worry

All surgeons have my deep respect,
And yet the honest fact is
I'd feel a lot less nervous if
They wouldn't call it "practice."

Nocturnal Note

Some people lie awake at night
Reviewing what went wrong;
I'd rather dwell on what went right—
It doesn't take as long.

Position Statement

This guy retired as President,
An act his wife deplored;
She knew he had no hobbies—now
He's chairman of the bored.

Knowledge Notice

Teach kids to love great poetry
And nature's wonders, please;
Take them aside and tell them all
About the bards and bees.

Sinful Syntax

Most ladies-of-the-evening are
Without much erudition—
They therefore end each sentence with,
Alas, a proposition.

Tress Truth

Some blondes are natural, of course,
And are acclaimed as beauts,
But other blondes get there, I fear,
By very different roots.

Position Statement

In stores, the naughty magazines
Are upside-down, I note,
So that they can't be seen by those
Not old enough to vote.
This practice is okay with me
And no tears do I shed,
But it is often why you'll see
Me standing on my head.

Cruise News

He owns a yacht and so a lot
Of women think he's great;
He's wed so often he cannot
Remember his first mate.

The Hull Truth

Boat owners scrape and chalk and paint
And then with sails they wrestle;
I makes me faint—I'm glad I ain't
A vassal to a vessel.

Challenging Choice

Our daughter's getting wed and this
Decision I've been dreading:
Do I give up my round of golf
Or do I tape the wedding?

Leg Lines

I think that I shall never see
A joint as homely as a knee;
To women also that applies,
But cheer up, guys! Knees lead to thighs!

Fourth Feeling

Hurrah for Thomas Jefferson,
Who helped to found our nation!
In fact, hurrah for everyone
Who signed the Declaration!
We honor all who waged the fight
And won our freedom dear,
But, thinking back to that dark night,
It's Paul whom we Revere!

Scarce Service

It's easy to identify
A weekend—that's no boast;
It's when some home appliance will
Have given up the ghost.

Outside Information

We send you smokers out of doors
And otherwise disown ya;
If you don't get lung cancer, you
Will freeze and get pneumonia.

Motor Matter

Cars built today can talk to you
And tell you what you didn't do;
Another gadget sounds alarms
Should your car be in burglar's arms;
With power buttons, shelf on shelf,
The darn thing nearly drives itself;
The auto-makers know high tech
And I would gladly write my check
For any car they bring to market
That comes with someplace I can park it.

Land Lament

There is a lovely piece of earth
Where trees grow straight and tall there;
It's where the animals give birth
And have themselves a ball there.
It's beautiful in wintertime
And summer, spring and fall there;
It is so nice, I'll bet a dime
Next month there'll be a mall there.

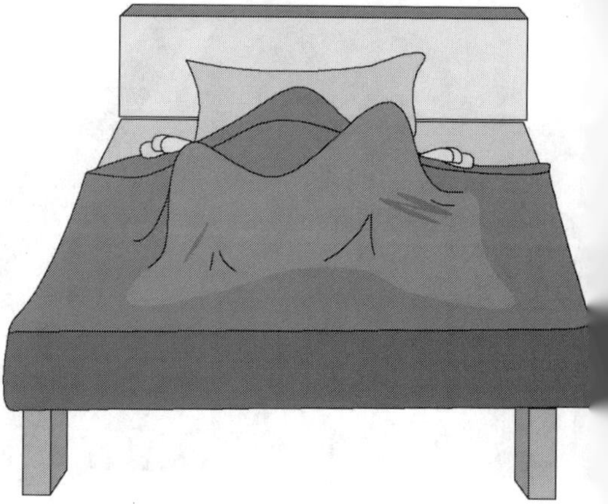

Snooze News

Some folks buy videos to watch;
That's not the path *I've* chosen;
I'd rather take a nap instead—
It's cheaper by the dozin'.

Seat of the Problem

Quite possibly it won't transpire,
But I will push my quest on
In hopes that one day I'll acquire
Some laurels I can rest on.

Winged Victory

Because of all the sex taboos
That we've been busy freeing,
The birds and bees now tell <u>their</u> young
About the human being.

Gum Lines

I asked my dentist what he thought
And told him where my doubt lay:
Which would be worse — the inlay
Or, later on, the outlay?

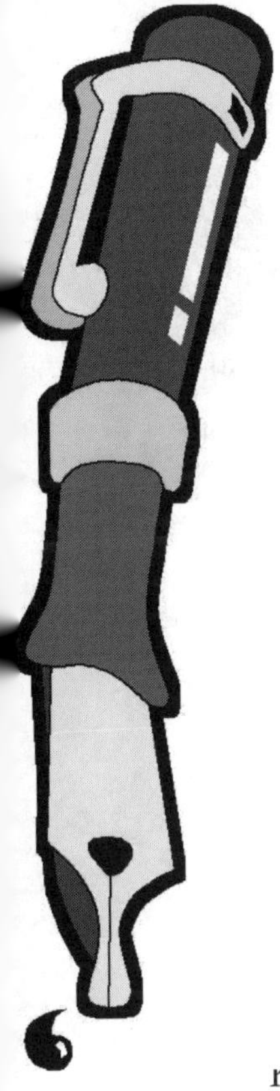

The Write Stuff

Banks brag about huge assets, but
To me that's simply murk;
I only want a bank in which
The lobby pens will work.

Puppy Love

Why is it dogs love little kids?
Well, these come to the fore:
Kids love to play and, what's more, they
Throw food upon the floor.

So Shoot Me

There's still one gunslinger out west
Who's not heard heaven's harp;
He is so old, I have been told,
They call him Wyatt AARP.

Closing Remarks

I know how I have signed this note,
The truth, though, it obscures;
In spite of what it says below,
I'm not sincerely yours.

Spanish Acquisition

Bullfighters, using skill and force,
Will earn a lusty cheer;
They'll kill the beast and then, of course,
Take home a souven-ear.

Bonnet Sonnet

Time was when ladies used to wear
To church a hat upon their hair;
Oh, glorious were they and flowery!
And some were wide and some were towery!
I liked the ones with ribbons best—
Or else the ones with birds in nest!
What fun to gaze upon a sea of 'em!
There wasn't one pew that was free of 'em!
Alas, the times they are a-changin',
And now a hat's what they look strange in;
Farewell to velvet, silk and ermine—
I guess I'll listen to the sermon.

View Point

The Scots who wear those gorgeous kilts
Are careful not to walk on stilts.

No Title

Since brevity's the soul of wit,
I quit.

Last Lines

My thanks for buying this small book!
I'm glad you didn't spurn it—
Or, if it's borrowed, take a look
And then, dear friend, return it.